THE MOST HILARIOUS

DONALD TRUMP TWEETS & QUOTES

The Ultimate Collection of the 45th President of the United
States' Tweets, Speeches, Gags and other Trumpisms

By

Andrew Fischer

As we all know, the 45th President of the USA loves social media. He also loves to talk.

Over the past 4 years of his presidency, Donald Trump has talked and commented and tweeted. He has talked at White House press conferences, he has talked at campaign after campaign and he has talked to other leaders while abroad. President Donald Trump was also never afraid to offer a piece of advice in public or on his Twitter account.

I read thousands of Trump's tweets and watched hours of his press conferences and other public appearances. In this book I've gathered the best of the best quotes and tweets of his 4 year-long presidency.

You will discover that Trump's quotes are sometimes quite funny and sometimes quite controversial. Other quotes are historic, touching and really memorable.

To commemorate the end of Trump's presidency, here are all of his famous tweets & quotes from January 2017 to January 2021.

Contents

TRUMP ON INTERNATIONAL POLITICS

"Before taking office people were assuming that we were going to War with North Korea. President Obama said that North Korea was our biggest and most dangerous problem. No longer - sleep well tonight!" (June 2018)

"For decades, politicians promised to secure the border, fix our trade deals, bring back our factories, get tough on China, move the Embassy to Jerusalem, make NATO pay their fair share, and so much else - only to do NOTHING (or worse)...." (January 2019)

"To Iranian President Rouhani: NEVER, EVER THREATEN THE UNITED STATES AGAIN OR YOU WILL SUFFER CONSEQUENCES THE LIKES OF WHICH FEW THROUGHOUT HISTORY HAVE EVER SUFFERED BEFORE. WE ARE NO LONGER A COUNTRY THAT WILL STAND FOR YOUR DEMENTED WORDS OF VIOLENCE & DEATH. BE CAUTIOUS!" (July 2018)

"North Korean Leader Kim Jong Un just stated that the "Nuclear Button is on his desk at all times." Will someone from his depleted and food starved regime please inform him that I too have a Nuclear Button, but it is a much bigger & more powerful one than his, and my Button works!" (January 2018)

"Why would Kim Jong-un insult me by calling me "old," when I would NEVER call him "short and fat?" Oh well, I try so hard to be his friend - and maybe someday that will happen!" (November 2017)

"After defeating 100% of the ISIS Caliphate, I largely moved our troops out of Syria. Let Syria and Assad protect the Kurds and fight Turkey for their own land. I said to my Generals, why should we be fighting for Syria...." (October 2019)

"I have been FAR tougher on Russia than Obama, Bush or Clinton. Maybe tougher than any other President. At the same time, & as I have often said, getting along with Russia is a good thing, not a bad thing. I fully expect that someday we will have good relations with Russia again!" (January 2019)

"Three individuals were sentenced to death in Iran for participating in protests. The execution is expected momentarily. Executing these three people sends a terrible signal to the world and should not be done!" (July 2020)

"So now Crooked Hillary is at it again! She is calling Congresswoman Tulsi Gabbard "a Russian favorite," and Jill Stein "a Russian asset." As you may have heard, I was called a big Russia lover also (actually, I do like Russian people. I like all people!). Hillary's gone Crazy!" (October 2019)

"Now the Fake News Media says I "pressured the Ukrainian President at least 8 times during my telephone call with him." This supposedly comes from a so-called "whistleblower" who they say doesn't even have a first hand account of what was said..." (September 2019)

"Congratulations Prime Minister Yoshihide Suga. You have a great life story! I know you will do a tremendous job for

Japan and for the world. Look forward to talking soon!"
(September 2020)

"Iran is in serious financial trouble. They want desperately to talk to the U.S., but are given mixed signals from all of those purporting to represent us, including President Macron of France" (August 2019)

"...I know the people of Puerto Rico well, and they are great. But much of their leadership is corrupt, & robbing the U.S. Government blind!" (July 2019)

"Mexico is doing great at the Border, but China is letting us down in that they have not been buying the agricultural products from our great Farmers that they said they would. Hopefully they will start soon!" (July 2019)

"People have been saying for years that we should talk to Mexico. The problem is that Mexico is an "abuser" of the United States, taking but never giving. It has been this way for decades..." (June 2019)

"In order not to pay Tariffs, if they start rising, companies will leave Mexico, which has taken 30% of our Auto Industry, and come back home to the USA. Mexico must take back their country from the drug lords and cartels. The Tariff is about stopping drugs as well as illegals!"
(May 2019)

"Mexico has taken advantage of the United States for decades. Because of the Dems, our Immigration Laws are BAD. Mexico makes a FORTUNE from the U.S., have for decades, they can easily fix this problem. Time for them to finally do what must be done!" (May 2019)

"90% of the Drugs coming into the United States come through Mexico & our Southern Border. 80,000 people died last year, 1,000,000 people ruined. This has gone on for many years & nothing has been done about it. We have a 100 Billion Dollar Trade Deficit with Mexico. It's time!"
(May 2019)

"Mexico's attitude is that people from other countries, including Mexico, should have the right to flow into the U.S. & that U.S. taxpayers should be responsible for the tremendous costs associated w/this illegal migration. Mexico is wrong and I will soon be giving a response!" (May 2019)

"It is very important for our Country's SECURITY that the United States Senate not vote for the Iran War Powers Resolution. We are doing very well with Iran and this is not the time to show weakness. Americans overwhelmingly support our attack on terrorist Soleimani..." (February 2020)

"....I will never stop working to secure the release of all Americans held hostage overseas! Thank you Switzerland for your great assistance." (June 2020)

"Just had a wonderful conversation with my friend, Prime Minister @AbeShinzo of Japan, who will be leaving office soon. Shinzo will soon be recognized as the greatest Prime Minister in the history of Japan, whose relationship with the USA is the best it has ever been. Special man!" (August 2020)

"I have asked Secretary of State Mike Pompeo not to go to North Korea, at this time, because I feel we are not making sufficient progress with respect to the denuclearization of the Korean Peninsula..." (August 2018)

"President Macron of France has just suggested that Europe build its own military in order to protect itself from the U.S., China and Russia. Very insulting, but perhaps Europe should first pay its fair share of NATO, which the U.S. subsidizes greatly!" (November 2018)

"I have confidence that Kim Jong Un will honor the contract we signed &, even more importantly, our handshake. We agreed to the denuclearization of North Korea. China, on the other hand, may be exerting negative pressure on a deal because of our posture on Chinese Trade-Hope Not!" (July 2018)

"Just spoke to President XI JINPING of China concerning the provocative actions of North Korea. Additional major sanctions will be imposed on North Korea today. This situation will be handled!" (November 2017)

"While I greatly appreciate the efforts of President Xi & China to help with North Korea, it has not worked out. At least I know China tried!" (June 2017)

"President Xi of China has been very helpful in his support of my meeting with Kim Jong Un. The last thing China wants are large scale nuclear weapons right next door. Sanctions placed on the border by China and Russia have been very helpful. Great relationship with Chairman Kim!" (February 2019)

"I am certain that, at some time in the future, President Xi and I, together with President Putin of Russia, will start talking about a meaningful halt to what has become a major and uncontrollable Arms Race. The U.S. spent 716 Billion Dollars this year. Crazy!" (December 2018)

"Hearing word that Russia, Syria and, to a lesser extent, Iran, are bombing the hell out of Idlib Province in Syria, and indiscriminately killing many innocent civilians. The World is watching this butchery. What is the purpose, what will it get you? STOP!" (June 2019)

"I was elected on getting out of these ridiculous endless wars, where our great Military functions as a policing operation to the benefit of people who don't even like the USA. The two most unhappy countries at this move are Russia & China, because they love seeing us bogged....." (October 2019)

"After defeating 100% of the ISIS Caliphate, I largely moved our troops out of Syria. Let Syria and Assad protect the Kurds and fight Turkey for their own land. I said to my Generals, why should we be fighting for Syria and Assad to protect the land of our enemy? Anyone who wants to assist Syria in protecting the Kurds is good with me, whether it is Russia, China, or Napoleon Bonaparte. I hope they all do great, we are 7,000 miles away!" (October 2019)

"For the record, I have no financial interests in Saudi Arabia (or Russia, for that matter). Any suggestion that I

have is just more FAKE NEWS (of which there is plenty)!"
(October 2018)

"What good is NATO if Germany is paying Russia billions of dollars for gas and energy? Why are there only 5 out of 29 countries that have met their commitment? The U.S. is paying for Europe's protection, then loses billions on Trade. Must pay 2% of GDP IMMEDIATELY, not by 2025."
(July 2018)

"Presidents have been trying unsuccessfully for years to get Germany and other rich NATO Nations to pay more toward their protection from Russia. They pay only a fraction of their cost. The U.S. pays tens of Billions of Dollars too much to subsidize Europe, and loses Big on Trade!" (July 2018)

"The threat from radical Islamic terrorism is very real, just look at what is happening in Europe and the Middle-East. Courts must act fast!" (February 2017)

"A new radical Islamic terrorist has just attacked in Louvre Museum in Paris. Tourists were locked down. France on edge again. GET SMART U.S." (February 2017)

"On Trade, France makes excellent wine, but so does the U.S. The problem is that France makes it very hard for the U.S. to sell its wines into France, and charges big Tariffs, whereas the U.S. makes it easy for French wines, and charges very small Tariffs. Not fair, must change!" (November 2018)

"If anybody but your favorite President, Donald J. Trump, announced that, after decimating ISIS in Syria, we were going to bring our troops back home (happy & healthy), that person would be the most popular hero in America. With me, hit hard instead by the Fake News Media. Crazy!" (December 2018)

"Spoke w/ President Erdogan of Turkey to advise where we stand on all matters including our last two weeks of success in fighting the remnants of ISIS, and 20 mile safe zone. Also spoke about economic development between the U.S. & Turkey - great potential to substantially expand!" (January 2019)

"....Likewise, do not want the Kurds to provoke Turkey. Russia, Iran and Syria have been the biggest beneficiaries of the long term U.S. policy of destroying ISIS in Syria - natural enemies. We also benefit but it is now time to bring our troops back home. Stop the ENDLESS WARS!" (January 2019)

"...almost 3 years, but it is time for us to get out of these ridiculous Endless Wars, many of them tribal, and bring our soldiers home. WE WILL FIGHT WHERE IT IS TO OUR BENEFIT, AND ONLY FIGHT TO WIN. Turkey, Europe, Syria, Iran, Iraq, Russia and the Kurds will now have to figure the situation out, and what they want to do with the captured ISIS fighters in their "neighborhood." They all hate ISIS, have been enemies for years. We are 7000 miles away and will crush ISIS again if they come anywhere near us!" (October 2019)

TRUMP ON OTHER POLITICIANS

"The Democrats and President Obama gave Iran 150 Billion Dollars and got nothing, but they can't give 5 Billion Dollars for National Security and a Wall?" (December 2018)

"Just out that the Obama Administration granted citizenship, during the terrible Iran Deal negotiation, to 2,500 Iranians - including to government officials. How big (and bad) is that?" (July 2018)

"Crazy Joe Biden is trying to act like a tough guy. Actually, he is weak, both mentally and physically, and yet he threatens me, for the second time, with physical assault. He doesn't know me, but he would go down fast and hard, crying all the way. Don't threaten people Joe!" (March 2018)

"Joe Biden should not wrongfully claim the office of the President. I could make that claim also. Legal proceedings are just now beginning!" (November 2020)

"The biggest loser tonight, by far, is Mini Mike Bloomberg. His "political" consultants took him for a ride. $700 million washed down the drain, and he got nothing for it but the nickname Mini Mike, and the complete destruction of his reputation. Way to go Mike!" (March 2020)

"[Kamala Harris] this monster that was onstage with Mike Pence, who destroyed her last night, by the way. I thought that wasn't even a contest last night. She was terrible. I don't think you could get worse. And totally unlikeable."
(2020)

"Crooked Hillary Clinton is the worst (and biggest) loser of all time. She just can't stop, which is so good for the Republican Party. Hillary, get on with your life and give it another try in three years!" (November 2017)

"Joe Biden is coming out of the basement earlier than his hoped for ten days because his people told him he has no choice, his poll numbers are PLUNGING! Going to Pittsburgh, where I have helped industry to a record last year, & then back to his basement for an extended period..." (August 2020)

"Joe Biden is the living embodiment of the corrupt political class that enriched itself while draining the economic life and soul from our Country. For the last 47 years, Joe Biden shipped away your jobs, shut down your factories, threw open your borders, and ravaged our cities while sacrificing American blood and treasure in endless foreign wars. Joe Biden is a corrupt politician — and the Biden family is a criminal enterprise. This makes Crooked Hillary Clinton look like amateur hour!" (October 2020)

"President Bush fired him also. Bolton is incompetent!" (June 2020)

"Being nice to Rocket Man hasn't worked in 25 years, why would it work now? Clinton failed, Bush failed, and Obama failed. I won't fail." (October 2017)

"From Bush 1 to present, our Country has lost more than 55,000 factories, 6,000,000 manufacturing jobs and accumulated Trade Deficits of more than 12 Trillion Dollars. Last year we had a Trade Deficit of almost 800 Billion Dollars. Bad Policies & Leadership. Must WIN again!" (March 2018)

"Looking forward to being with the wonderful Bush family at Blair House today. The former First Lady will be coming over to the White House this morning to be given a tour of the Christmas decorations by Melania. The elegance & precision of the last two days have been remarkable!" (December 2018)

"For 47 years, Joe Biden viciously attacked Black Americans. He called young black men "super predators." To every black American: I am asking for your vote. This is your one and only chance to show Sleepy Joe what you think of his decision to attack you, jail you, and betray you!" (November 2020)

"Just spoke with Prime Minister @BorisJohnson of the United Kingdom. Very thankful for his friendship and support as I recovered from the China Virus. I am looking forward to working with him for many years to come, a great guy!" (October 2020)

"Joe Biden is the candidate of rioters, looters, arsonists, gun-grabbers, flag-burners, Marxists, lobbyists, and special interests..." (November 2020)

"Joe Biden spent the last 47 years outsourcing your jobs, opening your borders, and sacrificing American blood and treasure in endless foreign wars. He is a diehard globalist who cares nothing for working people. He repeatedly tried to cut Medicare & Social Security" (October 2020)

"A vote for Joe Biden is a vote to extinguish and eradicate your state's auto industry. Biden is a corrupt politician who SOLD OUT Michigan to CHINA. Biden is the living embodiment of the decrepit and depraved political class that got rich bleeding America Dry!" (November 2020)

"Joe Biden is promising to delay the vaccine and turn America into a prison state—locking you in your home while letting far-left rioters roam free. The Biden Lockdown will mean no school, no graduations, no weddings, no Thanksgiving, no Christmas, no Fourth of July..." (November 2020)

"no future for America's youth. A vote for Biden is a vote for Lockdowns, Layoffs and Misery. Get out and VOTE tomorrow!" (November 2020)

"Biden and the Democrats want to get rid of the Private Healthcare Plans for 180 MILLION Americans that are happy. They'll be put on socialized medicine!" (September 2020)

"Biden will Shutdown the Economy at the tip of a hat, raise your Taxes, knock out your Second Amendment and Defund, or close, your Police. The Suburbs would be next, get ready. Also, and incredibly, PACK THE UNITED STATES SUPREME COURT. This is not what the USA wants!!!" (October 2020)

"Joe Biden is a corrupt politician. He wants to send YOUR jobs to China, while his family rakes in millions from the Chinese Communist Party. If Biden wins, China will OWN the USA. When we win, YOU win, Wisconsin wins, and AMERICA wins!" (October 2020)

"Biden wants to Pack the Supreme Court, thereby ruining it. Also, he wants no fracking, killing our Energy business, and JOBS. Second Amendment is DEAD if Biden gets in! Is that what you want from a leader? He will destroy our Country! VOTE NOW USA." (September 2020)

"Corrupt Joe Biden has confirmed that he "would give UNLIMITED Healthcare to Illegal Immigrants". This would break our system and bring millions of people to the USA." (June 2020)

"Crooked Hillary Clinton now blames everybody but herself, refuses to say she was a terrible candidate. Hits Facebook & even Dems & DNC." (June 2017)

"That shouldn't be hard. Corrupt Joe has done nothing good for Black people!" (July 2020)

"Joe Biden constantly used the term "Super Predator" when referring to young Black Men, according to my sources." (November 2020)

"Crazy Bernie Sanders recently equated the City of Baltimore to a THIRD WORLD COUNTRY! Based on that statement, I assume that Bernie must now be labeled a Racist, just as a Republican would if he used that term and standard! The fact is, Baltimore can be brought back, maybe......" (July 2019)

"One of the most important issues is LAW & ORDER. Biden stands with the rioters & looters - I stand with the HEROES of law enforcement. If Biden wins, the rioters in the streets will be running your federal government. No city, no family, and no community will be safe. VOTE #MAGA!" (October 2020)

"Why didn't President Obama do something about Russia in September (before November Election) when told by the FBI? He did NOTHING, and had no intention of doing anything!" (May 2019)

"...What about all of the Clinton ties to Russia, including Podesta Company, Uranium deal, Russian Reset, big dollar speeches etc." (July 2017)

"This Russian connection non-sense is merely an attempt to cover-up the many mistakes made in Hillary Clinton's losing campaign." (February 2017)

"So Biden is coughing and hacking and playing "fingers" with his mask, all over the place, and the Fake News doesn't want to even think about discussing it. "Journalism" has reached the all time low in history. Sadly, Lamestream knows this and doesn't even care!" (October 2020)

"While I travel the Country, Joe sleeps in his basement, telling the Fake News Media to "get lost". If you're a reporter covering Sleepy Joe, you have basically gone into retirement!" (September 2020)

"Joe Biden called me George yesterday. Couldn't remember my name..." (October 2020)

"Biden Works for Big Tech, Big Media — They Keep Scandals Quiet..." (October 2020)

"Media and Big Tech are not covering Biden Corruption!" (October 2020)

"Last night I did what the corrupt media has refused to do: I held Joe Biden Accountable for his 47 years of lies, 47 years of betrayals, and 47 years of failure. The whole nation saw the truth — Joe Biden is too weak to lead this Country!" (October 2020)

"Russian Billionaire wired Hunter Biden 3 1/2 Million Dollars. This on top of all of the other money he received while Joe was V.P...." (September 2020)

"Somebody please tell Congressman Clyburn, who doesn't have a clue, that the chart he put up indicating more CASES for the U.S. than Europe, is because we do MUCH MORE testing than any other country in the World. If we had no testing, or bad testing, we would show very few CASES" (July 2020)

"Joe Biden is bought and paid for by Big Tech, Big Media, Big Donors, and powerful special interests. They are desperate for him to win because they own him, they control him, and they know he will always do their bidding!" (November 2020)

"Fake Journalists!" (May 2020)

"Ask Sally Yates, under oath, if she knows how classified information got into the newspapers soon after she explained it to W.H. Counsel" (May 2017)

"We have made more progress in the last nine months against ISIS than the Obama Administration has made in 8 years.Must be proactive & nasty!" (September 2017)

"Welcome to the race Sleepy Joe. I only hope you have the intelligence, long in doubt, to wage a successful primary campaign. It will be nasty - you will be dealing with people who truly have some very sick & demented ideas. But if you make it, I will see you at the Starting Gate!" (April 2019)

"@SadiqKhan , who by all accounts has done a terrible job as Mayor of London, has been foolishly "nasty" to the visiting President of the United States, by far the most important ally of the United Kingdom. He is a stone cold loser who should focus on crime in London, not me..." (June 2019)

"Joe Biden's handling of the H1N1 Swine Flu was a complete and total disaster. Even polls on the matter were terrible!" (May 2020)

"Remember, I wouldn't be President now had Obama and Biden properly done their job. The fact is, they were TERRIBLE!!!" (October 2020)

"Bolton's book, which is getting terrible reviews, is a compilation of lies and made up stories, all intended to make me look bad. Many of the ridiculous statements he attributes to me were never made, pure fiction. Just trying to get even for firing him like the sick puppy he is!" (June 2018)

"Governor Whitmer of Michigan has done a terrible job. She locked down her state for everyone, except her husband's boating activities. The Federal Government provided tremendous help to the Great People of Michigan..." (October 2020)

"I was right about Comey, CROOKED COP!" (August 2019)

"Crooked Hillary caught again. She is a total train wreck!" (December 2019)

"Andy McCabe is a major sleazebag. Among many other things, he took massive amounts of money from Crooked Hillary reps, for wife's campaign, while Hillary was under "investigation" by FBI!" (July 2019)

"Corrupt politician Joe Biden makes Crooked Hillary look like an amateur!" (October 2018)

"Yesterday was a BIG day for Justice in the USA. Congratulations to General Flynn, and many others. I do believe there is MUCH more to come! Dirty Cops and Crooked Politicians do not go well together!" (May 2020)

"Was Andy McCabe ever forced to pay back the $700,000 illegally given to him and his wife, for his wife's political campaign, by Crooked Hillary Clinton while Hillary was under FBI investigation, and McCabe was the head of the FBI??? Just askin'?" (September 2020)

"Bernie Sanders, "The Economy is doing well, and I'm sure I don't have to give Trump any credit - I'm sure he'll take all the credit that he wants." Wrong Bernie, the Economy is doing GREAT, and would have CRASHED if my opponent (and yours), Crooked Hillary Clinton, had ever won!" (May 2019)

"So why didn't the highly conflicted Robert Mueller investigate how and why Crooked Hillary Clinton deleted and acid washed 33,000 Emails immediately AFTER getting a SUBPOENA from the United States Congress? She must have GREAT lawyers!" (July 2019)

"Everybody does phony books on Donald Trump and Republicans, just like the Fake Dossier, which turned out to be a total fraud perpetrated by Crooked Hillary Clinton and the DNC" (August 2020)

"Biden was asked questions at his so-called Press Conference yesterday where he read the answers from a teleprompter. That means he was given the questions, just like Crooked Hillary. Never have seen this before!" (July 2020)

"I think that Crooked Hillary Clinton should enter the race to try and steal it away from Uber Left Elizabeth Warren. Only one condition. The Crooked one must explain all of her high crimes and misdemeanors including how & why she deleted 33,000 Emails AFTER getting "C" Subpoena!" (October 2019)

"Washed up Creepster John Bolton is a lowlife who should be in jail, money seized, for disseminating, for profit, highly Classified information..." (June 2020)

"When will the Fake News Media start asking Democrats if they are OK with the hiring of Christopher Steele, a foreign agent, paid for by Crooked Hillary and the DNC, to dig up "dirt" and write a phony Dossier against the Presidential Candidate of the opposing party..."(June 2019)

"Obama, Biden, Crooked Hillary and many others got caught in a Treasonous Act of Spying and Government Overthrow, a Criminal Act. How is Biden now allowed to run for President?" (October 2020)

"So they now convict Roger Stone of lying and want to jail him for many years to come. Well, what about Crooked Hillary, Comey, Strzok, Page, McCabe, Brennan, Clapper, Shifty Schiff, Ohr & Nellie, Steele & all of the others, including even Mueller himself? Didn't they lie?"
(November 2019)

TRUMP ON TERRORISM

"Horrible and cowardly terrorist attack on innocent and defenseless worshipers in Egypt. The world cannot tolerate terrorism, we must defeat them militarily and discredit the extremist ideology that forms the basis of their existence!" (November 2017)

"...I want Russia to greatly step up their fight against ISIS & terrorism." (May 2017)

"The threat from radical Islamic terrorism is very real, just look at what is happening in Europe and the Middle-East. Courts must act fast!" (February 2017)

"Big G7 meetings today. Lots of very important matters under discussion. First on the list, of course, is terrorism..." (May 2017)

"Many reports of peaceful protests by Iranian citizens fed up with regime's corruption & its squandering of the nation's wealth to fund terrorism abroad. Iranian govt should respect their people's rights, including right to express themselves. The world is watching!..." (December 2017)

"When will all the haters and fools out there realize that having a good relationship with Russia is a good thing, not a bad thing. There always playing politics - bad for our country. I want to solve North Korea, Syria, Ukraine, terrorism, and Russia can greatly help!" (November 2017)

"Big protests in Iran. The people are finally getting wise as to how their money and wealth is being stolen and squandered on terrorism. Looks like they will not take it any longer. The USA is watching very closely for human rights violations!" (December 2017)

"The people of Iran are finally acting against the brutal and corrupt Iranian regime. All of the money that President Obama so foolishly gave them went into terrorism and into their "pockets." The people have little food, big inflation and no human rights. The U.S. is watching!" (January 2018)

". @Theresa_May, don't focus on me, focus on the destructive Radical Islamic Terrorism that is taking place within the United Kingdom. We are doing just fine!" (November 2017)

"So sad to hear of the terrorist attack in Egypt. U.S. strongly condemns..." (April 2017)

"Another attack in London by a loser terrorist. These are sick and demented people who were in the sights of Scotland Yard. Must be proactive!" (September 2017)

"The threat from radical Islamic terrorism is very real, just look at what is happening in Europe and the Middle-East. Courts must act fast!" (February 2017)

"Radical Islamic Terrorism must be stopped by whatever means necessary! The courts must give us back our protective rights. Have to be tough!" (August 2017)

"Horrible and cowardly terrorist attack on innocent and defenseless worshipers in Egypt. The world cannot tolerate terrorism, we must defeat them militarily and discredit the extremist ideology that forms the basis of their existence!" (November 2017)

"After historic victories against ISIS, it's time to bring our great young people home!" (December 2018)

"We have declassified a picture of the wonderful dog (name not declassified) that did such a GREAT JOB in capturing and killing the Leader of ISIS, Abu Bakr al-Baghdadi!" (October 2019)

"Big wins against ISIS!" (July 2017)

"Fighting between various groups that has been going on for hundreds of years. USA should never have been in Middle East. Moved our 50 soldiers out. Turkey MUST take over captured ISIS fighters that Europe refused to have returned. The stupid endless wars, for us, are ending!" (October 2019)

"Five Most Wanted leaders of ISIS just captured!" (May 2018)

"Getting out of Syria was no surprise. I've been campaigning on it for years, and six months ago, when I very publicly wanted to do it, I agreed to stay longer. Russia, Iran, Syria & others are the local enemy of ISIS. We were doing there work. Time to come home & rebuild...." (December 2018)

"ISIS has a new leader. We know exactly who he is!" (November 2019)

"I've done more damage to ISIS than all recent presidents....not even close!" (December 2018)

"We must not allow ISIS to return, or enter, our country after defeating them in the Middle East and elsewhere. Enough!"(October 2017)

"We have 1,800 ISIS Prisoners taken hostage in our final battles to destroy 100% of the Caliphate in Syria. Decisions are now being made as to what to do with these dangerous prisoners...." (April 2019)

"The Oil Fields discussed in my speech on Turkey/Kurds yesterday were held by ISIS until the United States took them over with the help of the Kurds. We will NEVER let a reconstituted ISIS have those fields!" (October 2019)

"NYC terrorist was happy as he asked to hang ISIS flag in his hospital room. He killed 8 people, badly injured 12. SHOULD GET DEATH PENALTY!" (November 2017)

"We defeated 100% of the ISIS Caliphate and no longer have any troops in the area under attack by Turkey, in Syria. We did our job perfectly! Now Turkey is attacking the Kurds, who have been fighting each other for 200 years...." (October 2019)

"ISIS just claimed the Degenerate Animal who killed, and so badly wounded, the wonderful people on the West Side, was "their soldier. Based on that, the Military has hit ISIS "much harder" over the last two days. They will pay a big price for every attack on us!" (November 2017)

"When I became President, ISIS was out of control in Syria & running rampant. Since then tremendous progress made, especially over last 5 weeks. Caliphate will soon be destroyed, unthinkable two years ago. Negotiating are proceeding well in Afghanistan after 18 years of fighting.. " (January 2019)

"If anybody but Donald Trump did what I did in Syria, which was an ISIS loaded mess when I became President, they would be a national hero. ISIS is mostly gone, we're slowly sending our troops back home to be with their families, while at the same time fighting ISIS remnants......" (December 2018)

"The United States of America will be designating ANTIFA as a Terrorist Organization." (May 2020)

"Five Most Wanted leaders of ISIS just captured!" (May 2018)

"Loser terrorists must be dealt with in a much tougher manner. The internet is their main recruitment tool which we must cut off & use better!" (September 2017)

TRUMP ON COVID

"The virus will not have a chance against us. No nation is more prepared or more resilient than the United States." (March 2020)

"I'm a little upset with China, I'll be honest with you." (March 2020)

"I think we have one of the lowest mortality rates"

"China has been working very hard to contain the Coronavirus. The United States greatly appreciates their efforts and transparency. It will all work out well"

"This is a flu" (February 2020)

"This is like a flu" (February 2020)

"I want every American to be prepared for the hard days that lie ahead [...] It's not the flu. It's vicious"

"Covid-19 will go away like a miracle"

"It's going to disappear one day, it's like a miracle, it will disappear" (February 2020)

"It was released [Covid-19] by China"

"This is China's fault"

"I just don't want to wear one myself [mask]. It's a recommendation, they recommend it"

"I think wearing a face mask as I greet presidents, prime ministers, dictators, kings, queens, I don't know somehow I don't see it for myself"

"It will probably unfortunately get worse before it gets better"

"I think that the World Health Organization should be ashamed of themselves, because they're like the public relations agency of China"

"We have it totally under control. It's one person coming in from China. We have it under control, it's going to be just fine" (January 2020)

"And then I see the disinfectant, it knocks it out in a minute. One minute. And is there a way we can do something like that by injection inside or almost a cleaning? Because you see it gets in the lungs and it does a tremendous number on the lungs, so it'd be interesting to check that." (April 2020)

"This is nobody's fault but China"

"I am for masks, I think masks are good. People have seen me wearing one"

"Looks like by April, you know, in theory, when it gets a little warmer, it miraculously goes away"

"I've always known this is a real, this is a pandemic. I've felt it was a pandemic long before it was called a pandemic" (March 2020)

"So, supposing we hit the body with a tremendous, whether it's ultraviolet or just very powerful light, and I think you said, that hasn't been checked but you're gonna test it. And then I said, supposing it brought the light inside the body, which you can do either through the skin or some other way"

"My Campaign spent a lot of money up front in order to compensate for the false reporting and Fake News concerning our handling of the China Virus. Now they see the GREAT job we have done, and we have 3 times more than we had 4 years ago - & are up in polls. Lots of $'s & ENERGY! " (September 2020)

"The 15 [Covid-19 cases in the USA] within a couple of days is going to be down to close to zero" (February 2020)

"America will again, and soon, be open for business. Very soon, a lot sooner than three or four months that somebody was suggesting"

"They have studied it. They know very much. In fact, we're very close to a vaccine" (February 2020)

"I think we're doing a really good job in this country at keeping it down, a tremendous job at keeping it down" (March 2020)

"I like this stuff. I really get it [how Covid-19 works]. People are surprised that I understand it... Every one of these doctors said, 'How do you know so much about this?' Maybe I have a natural ability. Maybe I should have done that instead of running for president." (March 2020)

"No, I'm not concerned at all"

"Relax"

"This is a very contagious virus. It's incredible. But it's something that we have tremendous control over"

"We cannot let the cure be worse than the problem itself"

"Don't forget, we have more cases than anybody in the world. But why? Because we do more testing"

"We've done a GREAT job on Covid response, making all Governors look good, some fantastic (and that's OK), but the Lamestream Media doesn't want to go with that narrative, and the Do Nothing Dems talking point is to say only bad about "Trump". I made everybody look good, but me!" (May 2020)

"When we have a lot of cases, I don't look at that as a bad thing. I look at that as, in a certain respect, as being a good thing...Because it means our testing is much better"

"And it is dying out. The numbers are starting to get very good" (June 2020)

"The number of China Virus cases goes up, because of great testing" (June 2020)

"Stay calm, it will go away. You know it"

"I couldn't have done it any better" [Trump's evaluation of his coronavirus response] (April 2020)

"When somebody is the president of the United States, the authority is total"

"You see states are starting to open up now, and it's very exciting to see" (April 2020)

"Coronavirus deaths are way down. Mortality rate is one of the lowest in the World. Our economy is roaring back and will not be shut down"

"America will develop a vaccine very soon, and we will defeat the virus. We will have it delivered in record time" (July 2020)

"There will be a vaccine before the end of the year and maybe even before November 1. I think we can probably have it sometime in October" (September 2020)

"We're rounding the corner. And, very importantly, vaccines are coming, but we're rounding the corner regardless" (September 2020)

"I went through it [Covid-19]. Now, they say I'm immune. I feel so powerful"

"If I listened totally to the scientists, we would right now have a country that would be in a massive depression instead" (October 2020)

"People are saying whatever. Just leave us alone. They're tired of it. People are tired of hearing Fauci and all these idiots"

"We have made tremendous progress with the China Virus, but the fake news refuses to talk about it this close to the election" (October 2020)

"You have to be calm. It'll go away"

"Anybody right now, and yesterday, anybody that needs a test gets a test. They're there. And the tests are beautiful...the tests are all perfect"

"We have a perfectly coordinated and fine-tuned plan at the White House for our attack on Corona Virus"

"It's going away. We want it to go away with very, very few deaths"

"I don't take responsibility at all"

"I take full responsibility"

"I'd rate it a ten" [Trump's rating of his Covid-19 response] (March 2020)

"The United States shows more CASES than other countries, which the Lamestream Fake News Media pounces on daily, because it TESTS at such a high (and costly) level. No country in the world tests at this level. The more you TEST, the more CASES you will be reporting. Very simple!" (October 2020)

"The Fake News is talking about CASES, CASES, CASES. This includes many low risk people. Media is doing everything possible to create fear prior to November 3rd. The Cases are up because TESTING is way up, by far the most, and best, in the world. Mortality rate is DOWN 85% plus!" (October 2020)

"I ask all Americans to band together and support your neighbors by not hoarding unnecessary amounts of food and essentials. TOGETHER we will stay STRONG and overcome this challenge!" (March 2020)

"I want all Americans to understand: we are at war with an invisible enemy, but that enemy is no match for the spirit and resolve of the American people..." (March 2020)

"I will be lowering the flags on all Federal Buildings and National Monuments to half-staff over the next three days in memory of the Americans we have lost to the CoronaVirus...." (May 2020)

"So last year 37,000 Americans died from the common Flu. It averages between 27,000 and 70,000 per year. Nothing is shut down, life & the economy go on. At this moment there are 546 confirmed cases of CoronaVirus, with 22 deaths. Think about that!" (March 2020)

"With the exception of New York & a few other locations, we've done MUCH better than most other Countries in dealing with the China Virus. Many of these countries are now having a major second wave. The Fake News is working overtime to make the USA (& me) look as bad as possible!" (August 2020)

"STOCK MARKET UP BIG, VACCINE COMING SOON. REPORT 90% EFFECTIVE. SUCH GREAT NEWS!" (November 2020)

"Tonight, @FLOTUS and I tested positive for COVID-19. We will begin our quarantine and recovery process immediately. We will get through this TOGETHER!" (October 2020)

TRUMP ON HIMSELF

"I'm nice to a lot of people. People don't understand that."
(September 2019)

"...I know tech better than anyone, & technology"
(December 2018)

"What do I know about branding, maybe nothing (but I did become President!), but if I were Boeing, I would FIX the Boeing 737 MAX, add some additional great features, & REBRAND the plane with a new name. No product has suffered like this one. But again, what the hell do I know?"
(April 2019)

"Years ago the Democrats had the money to build the Wall, but they didn't have any idea how to get it done. I am building it bigger and better than ever thought possible!"
(February 2020)

"I am the least racist president ever to serve in office"

"I WON THIS ELECTION, BY A LOT!" (November 2020)

"71,000,000 Legal Votes. The most EVER for a sitting President!" (November 2020)

"The Fake News Media, just like Election time 2016, is bringing up my Taxes & all sorts of other nonsense with illegally obtained information & only bad intent. I paid many millions of dollars in taxes but was entitled, like everyone else, to depreciation & tax credits....."
(September 2020)

"...Your hopes are my hopes, your dreams are my dreams, and your future is what I am fighting for every single day!" (November 2020)

"As long as I am President, I will always stand with the HEROES of Law Enforcement! Joe Biden won't." (October 2020)

"As long as I am President, America will NEVER be a socialist Country!" (October 2020)

"As long as I am President, we will remain the number one producer of oil and natural gas on earth – and we will remain Energy Independent!" (November 2020)

"Virginia Voters! Your Governor wants to obliterate your Second Amendment. I have stopped him. I am the only thing between you and your Second Amendment..." (October 2020)

"...We will do nothing to hurt our great Military professionals & heroes as long as I am your President." (August 2020)

"...I am saving the Suburbs - the American Dream! I terminated the Regulation that would bring projects and crime to Suburbia...." (October 2020)

"...I am lowering drug prices massively, 50% and more! Biden and Obama said they would do this for eight years, but never did" (July 2020)

"...I am the only President on record to give up my yearly $400,000 plus Presidential Salary!" (September 2020)

"...I am fighting for citizens of every race, color and creed..." (November 2020)

"...I am the candidate of farmers, factory workers, police officers, and hard-working, law-abiding patriots of every race, religion and creed!" (November 2020)

"...my Administration is achieving things that have never been done before, including unleashing perhaps the Greatest Economy in our Country's history" (May 2019)

"I am standing up to the global special interests who got rich bleeding America Dry. The corrupt establishment hates me because I don't answer to THEM – I answer to YOU!" (November 2020)

"I did more in 47 months than Biden did in 47 years. A VOTE for Republicans is a VOTE for SAFE communities, great JOBS, and a limitless FUTURE for ALL AMERICANS!" (October 2020)

"...I know what's good and bad, I'd be a pretty good reporter..." (February 2017)

"Who can figure out the true meaning of "covfefe" ??? Enjoy!" (May 2017)

"Lowest rated Oscars in HISTORY. Problem is, we don't have Stars anymore - except your President (just kidding, of course)!" (March 2018)

TRUMP ON CHINA

"CHINA!"

"One of the many great things about our just signed giant Trade Deal with China is that it will bring both the USA & China closer together in so many other ways. Terrific working with President Xi, a man who truly loves his country. Much more to come!" (January 2020)

"Over the next 4 years, we will make America into the Manufacturing Superpower of the World & end our reliance on China" (November 2020)

"We have made tremendous progress with the China Virus, but the Fake News refuses to talk about it this close to the Election" (October 2020)

"My highly regarded Executive Order protected 525,000 American jobs during the height of the Chinese Plague. Democrats want to have Open Borders!" (October 2020)

"Just In: Chinese State Media and Leaders of CHINA want Biden to win "the U.S. Election". If this happened (which it won't), China would own our Country, and our Record Setting Stock Markets would literally CRASH!" (August 2020)

"And, honestly, I think, as tough as this negotiation was, I think our relationship with China now might be the best it's been in a long, long time. And now it's reciprocal. Before, we were being ripped off badly. Now we have a reciprocal relationship, maybe even better than reciprocal for us" (January 2020)

"China has been working very hard to contain the Coronavirus. The United States greatly appreciates their efforts and transparency. It will all work out well. In particular, on behalf of the American People, I want to thank President Xi!" (January 2020)

"I just spoke to President Xi last night, and, you know, we're working on the — the problem, the virus. It's a —

it's a very tough situation. But I think he's going to handle it. I think he's handled it really well. We're helping wherever we can" (February 2020)

"Just had a long and very good conversation by phone with President Xi of China. He is strong, sharp and powerfully focused on leading the counterattack on the Coronavirus. He feels they are doing very well, even building hospitals in a matter of only days" (February 2020)

"I am running for re-election to bring prosperity to Nevada, to put violent criminals behind bars, and to ensure the future belongs to AMERICA—NOT China. If we win, AMERICA WINS! If Biden wins, China wins. If Biden Wins, the rioters, anarchists, and arsonists win. VOTE!" (September 2020)

"While I greatly appreciate the efforts of President Xi & China to help with North Korea, it has not worked out. At least I know China tried!" (June 2017)

"I know President Xi of China very well. He is a great leader who very much has the respect of his people. He is also a good man in a "tough business." I have ZERO doubt that if President Xi wants to quickly and humanely solve the Hong Kong problem, he can do it. Personal meeting?" (August 2019)

"Asian Americans are VERY angry at what China has done to our Country, and the World. Chinese Americans are the most angry of all. I don't blame them!" (May 2020)

"I have taken the toughest-ever action to stand up to China's rampant theft of Michigan jobs. Sleepy Joe Biden has vowed to remove those Tariffs and allow China to resume its pillaging. Joe Biden's Agenda is Made in China, my agenda is Made in the USA!" (September 2020)

"As I watch the Pandemic spread its ugly face all across the world, including the tremendous damage it has done to the USA, I become more and more angry at China. People can see it, and I can feel it!" (July 2020)

"China already charges a ta)x of 16% on soybeans. Canada has all sorts of trade barriers on our Agricultural products. Not acceptable!" (June 2018)

"If the U.S. sells a car into China, there is a tax of 25%. If China sells a car into the U.S., there is a tax of 2%. Does anybody think that is FAIR? The days of the U.S. being ripped-off by other nations is OVER!" (September 2018)

"All of the fools that are so focused on looking only at Russia should start also looking in another direction, China. But in the end, if we are smart, tough and well prepared, we will get along with everyone!" (August 2018)

".....China has been taking advantage of the United States on Trade for many years. They also know that I am the one that knows how to stop it. There will be great and fast economic retaliation against China if our farmers, ranchers and/or industrial workers are targeted!" (September 2018)

""Report just out: "China hacked Hillary Clinton's private Email Server." Are they sure it wasn't Russia (just kidding!)? What are the odds that the FBI and DOJ are right on top of this? Actually, a very big story. Much classified information!" " (August 2018)

"Farmers have not been doing well for 15 years. Mexico, Canada, China and others have treated them unfairly. By the time I finish trade talks, that will change. Big trade barriers against U.S. farmers, and other businesses, will finally be broken. Massive trade deficits no longer!" (June 2018)

"The Wall Street Journal has it wrong, we are under no pressure to make a deal with China, they are under pressure to make a deal with us. Our markets are surging, theirs are collapsing. We will soon be taking in Billions in Tariffs & making products at home. If we meet, we meet?" (September 2018)

"Our Intelligence has informed us that the Chinese Government is moving troops to the Border with Hong Kong. Everyone should be calm and safe!" (August 2019)

"Chinese Telecom Giant Huawei hires former Obama Cyber Security Official as a lobbyist. This is not good, or acceptable! @FoxNews @SteveHiltonx" (April 2019)

"Melania and I look forward to being with President Xi & Madame Peng Liyuan in China in two weeks for what will hopefully be a historic trip!" (October 2017)

"Leaving South Korea now heading to China. Looking very much forward to meeting and being with President Xi!" (November 2017)

"President Xi and I will always be friends, no matter what happens with our dispute on trade. China will take down its Trade Barriers because it is the right thing to do. Taxes will become Reciprocal & a deal will be made on Intellectual Property. Great future for both countries!" (April 2018)

"It was a great honor to have President Xi Jinping and Madame Peng Liyuan of China as our guests in the United States...." (April 2017)

"The failing @nytimes hates the fact that I have developed a great relationship with World leaders like Xi Jinping, President of China....." (November 2017)

"Please do not forget the great help that my good friend, President Xi of China, has given to the United States, particularly at the Border of North Korea. Without him it would have been a much longer, tougher, process!" (April 2018)

"Chinese President XI JINPING and I spoke at length about the meeting with KIM JONG UN of North Korea. President XI told me he appreciates that the U.S. is working to solve the problem diplomatically rather than going with the ominous alternative. China continues to be helpful!" (March 2018)

"I know President Xi of China very well. He is a great leader who very much has the respect of his people. He is also a good man in a "tough business." I have ZERO doubt that if President Xi wants to quickly and humanely solve the Hong Kong problem, he can do it. Personal meeting?" (August 2019)

"Very thankful for President Xi of China's kind words on tariffs and automobile barriers...also, his enlightenment on intellectual property and technology transfers. We will make great progress together!" (April 2018)

"I say openly to President Xi & all of my many friends in China that China will be hurt very badly if you don't make a deal because companies will be forced to leave China for other countries. Too expensive to buy in China. You had a great deal, almost completed, & you backed out!" (May 2019)

"President Xi and I have a very strong and personal relationship. He and I are the only two people that can bring about massive and very positive change, on trade and far beyond, between our two great Nations. A solution

for North Korea is a great thing for China and ALL!"
(December 2018)

"All of the fools that are so focused on looking only at Russia should start also looking in another direction, China. But in the end, if we are smart, tough and well prepared, we will get along with everyone!" (August 2018)

TRUMP ON RUSSIA

"You mean they are just now finding votes in Florida and
Georgia – but the Election was on Tuesday? Let's blame
the Russians and demand an immediate apology from
President Putin!" (November 2018)

"I don't know Putin, have no deals in Russia, and the
haters are going crazy - yet Obama can make a deal with
Iran, #1 in terror, no problem!" (February 2017)

"Had a long and very good conversation with President
Putin of Russia. As I have always said, long before the
Witch Hunt started, getting along with Russia, China, and
everyone is a good thing, not a bad thing...." (May 2019)

"The meeting between President Putin and myself was a
great success, except in the Fake News Media!" (July 2018)

"I called President Putin of Russia to congratulate him on
his election victory (in past, Obama called him also). The

Fake News Media is crazed because they wanted me to excoriate him. They are wrong! Getting along with Russia (and others) is a good thing, not a bad thing......."(March 2018)

"Many dead, including women and children, in mindless CHEMICAL attack in Syria. Area of atrocity is in lockdown and encircled by Syrian Army, making it completely inaccessible to outside world. President Putin, Russia and Iran are responsible for backing Animal Assad. Big price..." (April 2018)

"Very good call yesterday with President Putin of Russia. Tremendous potential for a good/great relationship with Russia, despite what you read and see in the Fake News Media. Look how they have misled you on "Russia Collusion." The World can be a better and safer place. Nice!" (May 2019)

"Sanctions were not discussed at my meeting with President Putin. Nothing will be done until the Ukrainian & Syrian problems are solved!" (July 2017)

"I strongly pressed President Putin twice about Russian meddling in our election. He vehemently denied it. I've already given my opinion....." (July 2017)

"Putin & I discussed forming an impenetrable Cyber Security unit   so that election hacking, & many other negative things, will be guarded.." (July 2017)

"I had a GREAT meeting with Putin and the Fake News used every bit of their energy to try and disparage it. So bad for our country!" (July 2018)

"Some people HATE the fact that I got along well with President Putin of Russia. They would rather go to war than see this. It's called Trump Derangement Syndrome!" (July 2018)

"While I had a great meeting with NATO, raising vast amounts of money, I had an even better meeting with

Vladimir Putin of Russia. Sadly, it is not being reported that way - the Fake News is going Crazy!" (July 2018)

"Congratulations to France, who played extraordinary soccer, on winning the 2018 World Cup. Additionally, congratulations to President Putin and Russia for putting on a truly great World Cup Tournament -- one of the best ever!" (July 2018)

"I got severely criticized by the Fake News Media for being too nice to President Putin. In the Old Days they would call it Diplomacy. If I was loud & vicious, I would have been criticized for being too tough. Remember when they said I was too tough with Chairman Kim? Hypocrites!" (July 2018)

"The Fake News Media wants so badly to see a major confrontation with Russia, even a confrontation that could lead to war. They are pushing so recklessly hard and hate the fact that I'll probably have a good relationship with Putin. We are doing MUCH better than any other country!" (July 2018)

"So many people at the higher ends of intelligence loved my press conference performance in Helsinki. Putin and I discussed many important subjects at our earlier meeting. We got along well which truly bothered many haters who wanted to see a boxing match. Big results will come!" (July 2018)

"Highly respected Senator Richard Burr, head of Senate Intelligence, said, after interviewing over 200 witnesses and studying over 2 million pages of documents, "WE HAVE FOUND NO COLLUSION BETWEEN THE TRUMP CAMPAIGN AND RUSSIA." The Witch Hunt, so bad for our Country, must end!" (February 2019)

"Russia and Ukraine just swapped large numbers of prisoners. Very good news, perhaps a first giant step to peace. Congratulations to both countries!" (September 2019)

"The end result of the greatest Witch Hunt in U.S. political history is No Collusion with Russia (and No Obstruction). Pretty Amazing!" (April 2019)

"Had a long and very good conversation with President Putin of Russia. As I have always said, long before the Witch Hunt started, getting along with Russia, China, and everyone is a good thing, not a bad thing...." (May 2019)

"So now Crooked Hillary is at it again! She is calling Congresswoman Tulsi Gabbard "a Russian favorite," and Jill Stein "a Russian asset." As you may have heard, I was called a big Russia lover also (actually, I do like Russian people. I like all people!). Hillary's gone Crazy!" (October 2019)

"The United States is learning much from the failed missile explosion in Russia. We have similar, though more advanced, technology. The Russian "Skyfall" explosion has people worried about the air around the facility, and far beyond. Not good!" (August 2019)

"Russia continues to say they had nothing to do with Meddling in our Election! Where is the DNC Server, and why didn't Shady James Comey and the now disgraced FBI agents take and closely examine it? Why isn't Hillary/Russia being looked at? So many questions, so much corruption!" (June 2018)

"Our relationship with Russia has NEVER been worse thanks to many years of U.S. foolishness and stupidity and now, the Rigged Witch Hunt!" (July 2018)

"I never said Russia did not meddle in the election, I said "it may be Russia, or China or another country or group, or it may be a 400 pound genius sitting in bed and playing with his computer." The Russian "hoax" was that the Trump campaign colluded with Russia - it never did!" (February 2018)

"We should start an immediate investigation into @SenSchumer and his ties to Russia and Putin. A total hypocrite!" (March 2017)

"Met with President Putin of Russia who was at #APEC meetings. Good discussions on Syria. Hope for his help to solve, along with China the dangerous North Korea crisis. Progress being made." (November 2017)

TRUMP ON AMERICA

"This election will decide whether we restore the rule of a corrupt political class – or whether we declare that in America, we are still governed by THE PEOPLE! Get out and VOTE!" (October 2020)

"Over the next 4 years, we will make America into the Manufacturing Superpower of the World & end our reliance on China. We will end surprise medical billing, require price transparency, lower drug prices even more, and we will always protect patients with pre-existing conditions!" (November 2020)

"Thanks to our pro-worker, pro-American economic policies, unemployment is at the lowest level in more than 50 years. We have created over 7 MILLION new JOBS. More Americans are working today than EVER before. We have the hottest ECONOMY on earth!" (January 2020)

"Americans are the strongest and most resilient people on earth...We will remove or eliminate every obstacle necessary to deliver our people the care that they need,

and that they are entitled to. No resource will be spared."
(March 2020)

"...Americans should be taught to take PRIDE in our Great
Country, and if you don't, there's nothing in it for you!"
(September 2020)

"...I do not tolerate ANY extreme violence. Defending ALL
Americans, even those who oppose and attack me, is what
I will always do as your President! Governor Whitmer—
open up your state, open up your schools, and open up
your churches!" (October 2020)

"33.1% GDP - BEST IN USA HISTORY. IF I AM ELECTED,
NEXT YEAR WILL BE OUR BEST EVER!" (October 2020)

"NASDAQ HITS ALL-TIME HIGH. Tremendous progress
being made, way ahead of schedule. USA!" (June 2020)

"Great job by @elonmusk in agreeing to build, in TEXAS, what is expected to be the largest auto plant anywhere in the world. He kept his word to me. Texas & @Tesla are big winners. MADE IN THE USA!" (July 2020)

"Stock Market up almost 40% since the Election, with 7 Trillion Dollars of U.S. value built throughout the economy. Lowest unemployment rate in many decades, with Black & Hispanic unemployment lowest in History, and Female unemployment lowest in 21 years. Highest confidence ever!" (June 2018)

"We will never be a Socialist or Communist Country. IF YOU ARE NOT HAPPY HERE, YOU CAN LEAVE! It is your choice, and your choice alone. This is about love for America. Certain people HATE our Country...." (July 2019)

"ISIS is in retreat, our economy is booming, investments and jobs are pouring back into the country, and so much more! Together there is nothing we can't overcome--even a very biased media. We ARE Making America Great Again!" (January 2018)

"We will be ending the AIDS epidemic shortly in America and curing childhood cancer very shortly" (August 2019)

"STOP THE COUNT!" (November 2020)

"They are finding Biden votes all over the place — in Pennsylvania, Wisconsin, and Michigan. So bad for our Country!" (November 2020)

"The United States has spent EIGHT TRILLION DOLLARS fighting and policing in the Middle East. Thousands of our Great Soldiers have died or been badly wounded. Millions of people have died on the other side. GOING INTO THE MIDDLE EAST IS THE WORST DECISION EVER MADE IN THE HISTORY OF OUR COUNTRY! We went to war under a false & now disproven premise, WEAPONS OF MASS DESTRUCTION. There were NONE! Now we are slowly & carefully bringing our great soldiers & military home. Our focus is on the BIG PICTURE! THE USA IS GREATER THAN EVER BEFORE!" (October 2019)

"Everybody is so well unified and working so hard. It is a beautiful thing to see. They love our great Country. We will end up being stronger than ever before!" (March 2020)

"...Our Country now is breaking records in almost every category, from Stock Market to Military to Unemployment. We have prosperity & success like never before.." (August 2019)

"With Votes in the House tomorrow, Democrats want to make it harder for Presidents to defend America, and stand up to, as an example, Iran. Protect our GREAT COUNTRY!" (January 2020)

"The Wall is being rapidly built! The Economy is GREAT! Our Country is Respected again!" (April 2019)

"Economic numbers reach an all time high, the best in our Country's history. Great to be a part of something so good for so many!" (July 2019)

"The leaders of virtually every country that I met at the G-20 congratulated me on our great economy. Many countries are having difficulties on that score. We have the best economy anywhere in the world, with GREAT & UNLIMITED potential looking into the future!" (June 2019)

"Many incredible things are happening right now for our Country. After years of being ripped off by other nations on both Trade Deals and the Military, things are changing fast. Big progress is being made. America is respected again. KEEP AMERICA GREAT!" (August 2019)

"...our Vets are finally being taken care of and now have Choice, our Courts will have 145 great new Judges, and 2 Supreme Court Justices, got rid of the disastrous Individual Mandate & will protect Pre-Existing Conditions, drug prices down for first time in 51 years (& soon will drop much further), Right to Try, protecting your 2nd Amendment, big Tax & Reg Cuts, 3.2 GDP, Strong Foreign

Policy, & much much more that nobody else would have been able to do. Our Country is doing GREAT!" (May 2019)

"Together, our task is to strengthen our families, to build up our communities, to serve our citizens, and to celebrate AMERICAN GREATNESS as a shining example to the world...." (December 2017)

"Our first duty, and our highest loyalty, is to the citizens of the United States. We will not rest until our border is secure, our citizens are safe, and we finally end the immigration crisis once and for all." (June 2018)

"The Democrats, are saying loud and clear that they do not want to build a Concrete Wall - but we are not building a Concrete Wall, we are building artistically designed steel slats, so that you can easily see through it. It will be beautiful and, at the same time, give our Country the security that our citizens deserve. It will go up fast and save us BILLIONS of dollars a month once completed!" (December 2018)

TRUMP ON MEDIA

"FAKE NEWS!"

"...accurately. 90% of media coverage of my Administration is negative, despite the tremendously positive results we are achieving, it's no surprise that confidence in the media is at an all time low! I will not allow our great country to be sold out by anti-Trump haters in the dying newspaper industry..." (July 2018)

"If a Republican LIED like Biden and Harris do, constantly, the Lamestream Media would be calling them out at a level never recorded before. For one year they called for No Fracking and big Tax Increases. Now they each say opposite. Fake News is working overtime!" (October 2020)

" Big spike in the China Plague in Europe and other places that the Fake News used to hold up as examples of places that are doing well, in order to make the U.S look bad. Be strong and vigilant, it will run its course. Vaccines and cures are coming fast!" (October 2020)

" In 2016, the ABC News/Washington Post Poll was such a complete disaster that these two Fake News Organizations changed the numbers prior to the Election. Now these haters are trying the same thing, though on a lesser scale, again. Will have a bigger win than even 2016!" (October 2020)

"Fake News is at it again! They will take any statement from me, no matter how proper or well delivered, & systematically, in complete conjunction with all of their allies, dismantle it. With Biden, they only give him softballs, and let him read the answers from a teleprompter!" (September 2020)

"The Fake News refuses to cover the fact that GDP went up 33.1% for the 3rd Quarter, the best number by far in our Country's history!" (October 2020)

"The Fake News, @CNN , MSDNC, the failing @nytimes , and the rest, are working overtime spewing every lie in the book to make sure they can demean and disparage, at

the highest level possible, to try and win an election for a man who is totally unqualified to be your President, S.J."
(October 2020)

"We have made tremendous progress with the China Virus, but the Fake News refuses to talk about it this close to the Election. COVID, COVID, COVID is being used by them, in total coordination, in order to change our great early election numbers. Should be an election law violation!" (October 2020)

"I keep reading Fake News stories that my campaign is running low on money. Not true, & if it were so, I would put up money myself. The fact is that we have much more money than we had 4 years ago, where we spent much less money than Crooked Hillary, and still easily won, 306-223!" (October 2020)

"The Fake News Media refuses to discuss how good the Economy and Stock Market, including JOBS under the Trump Administration, are doing. We will soon be in RECORD TERRITORY. All they want to discuss is COVID 19, where they won't say it, but we beat the Dems all day long, also!!!" (October 2020)

"A massive Disinformation Campaign is going on by the Democrats, their partner, the Fake News Media, & Big Tech. They create false stories and then push them like has never been done before, even beyond the 2016 Campaign. It imperils our Country, and must stop now. Victory 2020!" (September 2020)

"SO MUCH FAKE NEWS! The Lamestream Media has gone absolutely insane because they realize we are winning BIG in all of the polls that matter. They write or show one false story after another. They are truly sick people..." (October 2020)

"The Fake News Media is riding COVID, COVID, COVID, all the way to the Election. Losers!" (October 2020)

"THE FAKE NEWS MEDIA IS THE REAL OPPOSITION PARTY!" (October 2020)

"Final RCP Polling Averages Had Hillary Clinton Winning MI, WI, and PA ... The Polls are Fake just like much of the reported news. I won it all against Crooked Hillary!" (October 2020)

"I am not just running against Biden, I am running against the Corrupt Media, the Big Tech Giants, and the Washington Swamp. It is time to send a message to these wealthy liberal hypocrites by delivering Joe Biden a THUNDERING defeat on November 3rd!" (October 2020)

"Because the CORRUPT MEDIA doesn't want to show all of our good work in that it will hurt the Radical Left's Election chances!" (September 2020)

"Ari, THE MEDIA IS CORRUPT, JUST LIKE OUR DEMOCRAT RUN BALLOT SYSTEM IS CORRUPT! Look at what's happening with Fake, Missing and Fraudulent Ballots all over the Country??? VOTE" (October 2020)

"The Democrats, together with the corrupt Fake News Media, have launched a massive Disinformation Campaign the likes of which has never been seen before. They will say anything, like their recent lies about me and the Military, and hope that it sticks" (September 2020)

"A massive Disinformation Campaign is going on by the Democrats, their partner, the Fake News Media, & Big Tech. They create false stories and then push them like has never been done before, even beyond the 2016 Campaign. It imperils our Country, and must stop now. Victory 2020!" (September 2020)

"Watching @FoxNews weekend anchors is worse than watching low ratings Fake News @CNN , or Lyin' Brian Williams (remember when he totally fabricated a War Story trying to make himself into a hero, & got fired. A very dishonest journalist!)..." (July 2019)

"Are the investigative "journalists" of the New York Times going to investigate themselves - who is the anonymous letter writer?" (September 2018)

"When are the Fake Journalists, who received unwarranted Pulitzer Prizes for Russia, Russia, Russia, and the Impeachment Scam, going to turn in their tarnished awards so they can be given to the real journalists who got it right. I'll give you the names, there are plenty of them!" (May 2020)

"One of the reasons that Fake News has become so prevalent & far reaching is the fact that corrupt "journalists" base their stories on SOURCES that they make up in order to totally distort a narrative or story..." (March 2020)

"Does anybody get the meaning of what a so-called Noble (not Nobel) Prize is, especially as it pertains to Reporters and Journalists? Noble is defined as, "having or showing fine personal qualities or high moral principles and ideals." Does sarcasm ever work?" (April, 2020)

"If I wanted to fire Robert Mueller in December, as reported by the Failing New York Times, I would have fired him. Just more Fake News from a biased newspaper!" (April, 2018)

"The Amazon Washington Post and three lowlife reporters, Matt Zapotosky, Josh Dawsey, and Carol Leonnig, wrote another Fake News story, without any sources (pure fiction), about Bill Barr & myself. We both deny this story, which they knew before they wrote it. A garbage newspaper!" (November 2019)

"Just revealed that the Failing and Desperate New York Times was feeding false stories about me, & those associated with me, to the FBI. This shows the kind of unprecedented hatred I have been putting up with for years with this Crooked newspaper. Is what they have done legal?..." (June, 2019)

"A poll should be done on which is the more dishonest and deceitful newspaper, the Failing New York Times or the Amazon (lobbyist) Washington Post! They are both a disgrace to our Country, the Enemy of the People, but I just can't seem to figure out which is worse?..." (June 2019)

"So much Fake News being put in dying magazines and newspapers. Only place worse may be @NBCNews , @CBSNews , @ABC and @CNN . Fiction writers!" (October 2017)

"Those that worked with me in this incredible Midterm Election, embracing certain policies and principles, did very well. Those that did not, say goodbye! Yesterday was such a very Big Win, and all under the pressure of a Nasty and Hostile Media!" (November 2018)

"Great News: The boring but very nasty magazine, The Atlantic, is rapidly failing, going down the tubes, and has just been forced to announce it is laying off at least 20% of its staff in order to limp into the future. This is a tough time to be in the Fake News Business!" (May 2020)

"Juan Williams at @FoxNews is so pathetic, and yet when he met me in the Fox Building lobby, he couldn't have been nicer as he asked me to take a picture of him and me for his family. Yet he is always nasty and wrong!" (August 2019)

"The Washington Post's @PhilipRucker (Mr. Off the
Record) & @AshleyRParker , two nasty lightweight
reporters, shouldn't even be allowed on the grounds of the
White House because their reporting is so DISGUSTING &
FAKE...." (September 2019)

"The Lamestream Media is not talking about what is
happening with the Stock Market and JOBS. Both are doing
GREAT! The Radical Left will destroy the USA. Be careful
what you wish for!" (July 2020)

"The USA doesn't have Freedom of the Press, we have
Suppression of the Story, or just plain Fake News. So much
has been learned in the last two weeks about how corrupt
our Media is, and now Big Tech, maybe even worse. Repeal
Section 230!" (October 2020)

"The Fake News Media is doing everything possible to stir
up and anger the pols and as many people as possible
seldom mentioning the fact that the Mueller Report had as
its principle conclusion the fact that there was NO

COLLUSION WITH RUSSIA. The Russia Hoax is dead!"
(April 2019)

"So funny that The New York Times & The Washington
Post got a Pulitzer Prize for their coverage (100%
NEGATIVE and FAKE!) of Collusion with Russia - And
there was No Collusion! So, they were either duped or
corrupt? In any event, their prizes should be taken away
by the Committee!" (March 2019)

"I have a great relationship with Angela Merkel of
Germany, but the Fake News Media only shows the bad
photos (implying anger) of negotiating an agreement -
where I am asking for things that no other American
President would ask for!" (June 2018)

"FIGHT THE CORRUPT FAKE NEWS MEDIA. VOTE!"
(October 2020)

TRUMP ON WOMEN

"A great & wonderful woman [Queen Elizabeth II)]!" (April 2020)

"He [Brett Kavanaugh] should sue the women, and all of those who illegally worked with them, for false and disgusting accusations!!!" (October 2020)

"I have done more for WOMEN than just about any President in HISTORY! As we celebrate the 100th Anniversary of women's voting rights, we should build a BEAUTIFUL STATUE in Washington D.C. to honor the many brave women who made this possible for our GREAT COUNTRY" (August 2020)

"Congratulations to the U.S. Women's Soccer Team on winning the World Cup! Great and exciting play. America is proud of you all!" (July 2019)

"Do you think Suburban Women want to Defund the Police? I don't think so" (June 2020)

"Women's unemployment rate is down to 3.6% - was 7.9% in January, 2011. Things are looking good!" (March 2019)

"Today, it was my great honor to sign a Presidential Memorandum launching the Women's Global Development and Prosperity Initiative" (February 2019)

"On International Women's Day, we honor women worldwide for their vital role in shaping and strengthening our communities, families, governments, and businesses..." (March 2019)

"Suburban Women are trending strongly to our campaign because they want SAFETY, SECURITY, and love the fact that I terminated the REGULATION that would destroy their neighborhood and with it, the American Dream. Biden would bring the REGULATION back in a MUCH stronger form!!!" (October 2020)

"...The U.S. strongly supports breast feeding but we don't believe women should be denied access to formula. Many women need this option because of malnutrition and poverty." (July 2018)

"...and by the way, women have the lowest unemployment numbers in many decades - at the highest pay ever. Proud of that!" (January 2019)

"Despite thousands of hours wasted and many millions of dollars spent, the Democrats have been unable to show any collusion with Russia - so now they are moving on to the false accusations and fabricated stories of women who I don't know and/or have never met. FAKE NEWS!" (December 2017)

"College educated women want safety, security and healthcare protections – very much along with financial and economic health for themselves and our Country. I supply all of this far better than any Democrat (for

decades, actually). That's why they will be voting for me!"
(October 2018)

"Phyllis George was a great person and a true pioneer for women in television. The NFL could not have made a better "pick" when they choose Phyllis to be the first woman to represent them. Also, a wonderful First Lady of Kentucky as the wife of Gov. John Y. Brown" (May 2020)

"....cameras running. Another False Accusation. Why doesn't @washingtonpost report the story of the women taking money to make up stories about me? One had her home mortgage paid off. Only @FoxNews so reported...doesn't fit the Mainstream Media narrative."
(February 2018)

"Great meeting with a wonderful woman today, former Secretary of State, Condoleezza Rice!" (March 2017)

"The Queen of Soul, Aretha Franklin, is dead. She was a great woman, with a wonderful gift from God, her voice. She will be missed!" (August 2018)

"A woman I don't know and, to the best of my knowledge, never met, is on the FRONT PAGE of the Fake News Washington Post saying I kissed her (for two minutes yet) in the lobby of Trump Tower 12 years ago. Never happened! Who would do this in a public space with live security" (February 2018)

"I never called Meghan Markle "nasty." Made up by the Fake News Media, and they got caught cold! Will @CNN , @nytimes and others apologize? Doubt it!" (June 2019)

"[About Alexandria Ocasio-Cortez] "This is not even a smart person, other than she's got a good line of stuff. I mean, she goes out and she yaps"" (2020)

TRUMP ON IMMIGRATION

"More troops being sent to the Southern Border to stop the attempted Invasion of Illegals, through large Caravans, into our Country. We have stopped the previous Caravans, and we will stop these also. With a Wall it would be soooo much easier and less expensive. Being Built!" (January 2019)

"There is right now a full scale manhunt going on in California for an illegal immigrant accused of shooting and killing a police officer during a traffic stop. Time to get tough on Border Security. Build the Wall!" (December 2018)

"BUILD A WALL & CRIME WILL FALL!" (January 2019)

"President and Mrs. Obama built/has a ten foot Wall around their D.C. mansion/compound. I agree, totally necessary for their safety and security. The U.S. needs the same thing, slightly larger version!" (December 2018)

"The Republican Senate just passed bipartisan humanitarian assistance for our Southern Border, 84-8! In addition to aid, Congress must close the catastrophic loopholes that are driving the Crisis. We must end incentives for Smuggling Children, Trafficking Women, and Selling Drugs." (June, 2019)

"Last week the Fake News said that a section of our powerful, under construction, Southern Border Wall "fell over", trying to make it sound terrible, except the reason was that the concrete foundation was just poured & soaking wet when big winds kicked in. Quickly fixed "forever"." (February 2020)

"Harry Reid was right in 1993, before he and the Democrats went insane and started with the Open Borders (which brings massive Crime) "stuff." Don't forget the nasty term Anchor Babies. I will keep our Country safe. This case will be settled by the United States Supreme Court!" (October 2018)

"Democrats, fix the laws. Don't RESIST. We are doing a far better job than Bush and Obama, but we need strength and security at the Border! Cannot accept all of the people trying to break into our Country. Strong Borders, No Crime!" (June 2018)

"Joe Biden would increase refugees from terrorist nations by 700%. His plan would overwhelm your communities and turn Michigan, Minnesota, Wisconsin and the entire Midwest into a refugee camp. I am protecting your families and keeping Radical Islamic Terrorists OUT of our Country!" (November 2020)

"The Democrats are trying to belittle the concept of a Wall, calling it old fashioned. The fact is there is nothing else's that will work, and that has been true for thousands of years. It's like the wheel, there is nothing better. I know tech better than anyone, & technology....." (December, 2018)

"Wall is moving along strong, tall and quickly. Thank you Jim for all of your help!" (February 2020)

"The WALL is well under construction. So far we're up to 129 miles, and by early next year we will have 500 miles completed!" (March 2020)

"The powerful Trump Wall is replacing porous, useless and ineffective barriers in the high traffic areas requested by Border Patrol. Illegal crossing are dropping as more and more Wall is being completed!" (January 2020)

"Wall is moving fast in Texas, Arizona, New Mexico and California. Great numbers at the Southern Border. Dems want people to just flow in. They want very dangerous open Borders!" (July 2020)

"Not my Wall, which will soon be finished (and Mexico will pay for the Wall!)..." (October 2020)

"As the Wall goes up, illegal crossings go down. This past week we built over 10 miles of Wall at our Southern

Border. We now have 256 miles of NEW Wall and we are on track to have 300 miles completed by the end of August!" (July 2020)

"A great time to have strong Borders, and we now have the strongest Borders in our history. 182 miles of Border Wall already built! Dems want Open Borders, let EVERYONE IN. No thanks!" (May 2020)

"I agree, unlike other states that are poorly run & managed, Texas is in great shape...and the Southern Border Wall, which is going up FAST, puts it in even better position!" (June 2020)

"Mexico is sadly experiencing very big Corona Virus problems, and now California, get this, doesn't want people coming over the Southern Border. A Classic! They are so lucky that I am their President. Border is very tight and the Wall is rapidly being built!" (May 2020)

"Rather hard to believe that @FoxNews didn't know that the Border Wall is well under construction, fully financed,

& already over 200 miles long? Will soon be finished! They just reported that "it is something that Dems are unlikely to budge on in this election year"" (June 2020)

"Mexico is doing a far better job than the Democrats on the Border. Thank you Mexico!" (July 2019)

"I am very disappointed that Mexico is doing virtually nothing to stop illegal immigrants from coming to our Southern Border where everyone knows that because of the Democrats, our Immigration Laws are totally flawed & broken..." (May 2019)

"I want to give the Democrats every last chance to quickly negotiate simple changes to Asylum and Loopholes. This will fix the Southern Border, together with the help that Mexico is now giving us. Probably won't happen, but worth a try. Two weeks and big Deportation begins!" (June 2019)

"As a sign of good faith, Mexico should immediately stop the flow of people and drugs through their country and to our Southern Border. They can do it if they want!" (June 2019)

"Congress - FIX OUR INSANE IMMIGRATION LAWS NOW!" (July 2018)

"Illegal immigration affects the lives of all Americans. Illegal Immigration hurts American workers, burdens American taxpayers, undermines public safety, and places enormous strain on local schools, hospitals and communities" (November 2018)

"Our first duty, and our highest loyalty, is to the citizens of the United States. We will not rest until our border is secure, our citizens are safe, and we finally end the immigration crisis once and for all." (June 2018)

"We don't want what is happening with immigration in Europe to happen with us!" (June 2018)

"We cannot allow all of these people to invade our Country. When somebody comes in, we must immediately, with no Judges or Court Cases, bring them back from where they came. Our system is a mockery to good immigration policy and Law and Order. Most children come without parents..." (June 2018)

"Please understand, there are consequences when people cross our Border illegally, whether they have children or not - and many are just using children for their own sinister purposes. Congress must act on fixing the DUMBEST & WORST immigration laws anywhere in the world! Vote "R"" (July 2018)

"For those who want and advocate for illegal immigration, just take a good look at what has happened to Europe over the last 5 years. A total mess! They only wish they had that decision to make over again." (October 2018)

"Democrats in Congress must no longer Obstruct - vote to fix our terrible Immigration Laws now. I am watching what is going on from Europe - it would be soooo simple to fix. Judges run the system and illegals and traffickers know how it works. They are just using children!" (July 2018)

"I don't care what the political ramifications are, our immigration laws and border security have been a complete and total disaster for decades, and there is no way that the Democrats will allow it to be fixed without a Government Shutdown..." (July 2018)

"Without a Wall there cannot be safety and security at the Border or for the U.S.A. BUILD THE WALL AND CRIME WILL FALL!" (January 2019)

"The building of the Wall on the Southern Border will bring down the crime rate throughout the entire Country!" (January 2019)

"Only fools, or people with a political agenda, don't want a Wall or Steel Barrier to protect our Country from Crime, Drugs and Human Trafficking. It will happen - it always does!" (January 2019)

TRUMP ON ENVIRONMENT

"A massive 200 Billion Dollar Sea Wall, built around New York to protect it from rare storms, is a costly, foolish & environmentally unfriendly idea that, when needed, probably won't work anyway. It will also look terrible. Sorry, you'll just have to get your mops & buckets ready!" (January 2019)

"...Look at China how filthy it is, look at Russia, look at India, it's filthy! The air is filthy!... " (October 2020)

"We have done an incredible job environmentally. We have the cleanest air, the cleanest water and the best carbon emission standards that we have seen in many many years." (October 2020)

"...We have the best lowest number in carbon emissions..." (October 2020)

"I know more about wind than you do [speaking to Biden]. It's extremely expensive, kills all the birds, it's very intermittent, it's got a lot of problems..." (October 2020)

"America is blessed with extraordinary energy abundance, including more than 250 years worth of beautiful clean coal. We have ended the war on coal, and will continue to work to promote American energy dominance!" (May 2018)

"1. Which country has the largest carbon emission reduction?

AMERICA!

2. Who has dumped the most carbon into the air?

CHINA!

3. 91% of the world's population are exposed to air pollution above the World Health Organization's suggested level.

NONE ARE IN THE U.S.A.!

4. The U.S. now leads the world in energy production... BUT...

5. Who's got the world's cleanest and safest air and water?

AMERICA!"

6. The Democrats' destructive "environmental" proposals will raise your energy bill and prices at the pump. Don't the Democrats care about fighting American poverty?

7. The badly flawed Paris Climate Agreement protects the polluters, hurts Americans, and cost a fortune. NOT ON MY WATCH!

8. I want crystal clean water and the cleanest and the purest air on the planet – we've now got that!

(September 2019)

"I am committed to keeping our air and water clean but always remember that economic growth enhances environmental protection. Jobs matter!" (April 2017)

"I am glad that my friend @EmmanuelMacron and the protestors in Paris have agreed with the conclusion I reached two years ago. The Paris Agreement is fatally flawed because it raises the price of energy for responsible countries while whitewashing some of the worst polluters in the world. I want clean air and clean water and have been making great strides in improving America's environment. But American taxpayers – and American workers – shouldn't pay to clean up others countries' pollution" (December 2018)

"I can't believe that Nancy Pelosi's District in San Francisco is in such horrible shape that the City itself is in violation of many sanitary & environmental orders, causing it to owe the Federal Government billions of dollars - and all she works on is Impeachment. We should all work together to clean up these hazardous waste and homeless sites before the whole city rots away. Very bad and dangerous conditions, also severely impacting the Pacific Ocean and water supply. Pelosi must work on this mess and turn her District around!" (October 2019)

""America: the Cleanest Air in the World - BY FAR!"" (October 2018)

TRUMP ON DEMOCRATS

"Democrats, fix the laws. Don't RESIST. We are doing a far better job than Bush and Obama, but we need strength and security at the Border! Cannot accept all of the people trying to break into our Country. Strong Borders, No Crime!" (June 2018)

"The greatest overreach in the history of our Country. The Dems are obstructing justice and will not get anything done. A big, fat, fishing expedition desperately in search of a crime, when in fact the real crime is what the Dems are doing, and have done!" (March 2019)

"Democrats are becoming the Party of late term abortion, high taxes, Open Borders and Crime" (January 2019)

"Our Country cannot survive as a Socialist Nation, and that's what the Democrats want it to be. The USA will never become a large scale version of Venezuela. All control is already being taken away from Sleepy Joe. He has Zero to say!!!" (October 2020)

"Democrats are "heartless". They don't want to give STIMULUS PAYMENTS to people who desperately need the money, and whose fault it was NOT that the plague came in from China. Go for the much higher numbers, Republicans, it all comes back to the USA anyway (one way or another!)." (September 2020)

"Radical Left Democrats are going CRAZY!" (September 2020)

"Democrats only want BAILOUT MONEY for Blue States that are doing badly. They don't care about the people, never did!" (September 2020)

"The Democrats never even mentioned the words LAW & ORDER at their National Convention. That's where they are coming from. If I don't win, America's Suburbs will be OVERRUN with Low Income Projects, Anarchists, Agitators, Looters and, of course, "Friendly Protesters"." (September 2020)

"Biden and Democrats just clarified the fact that they are fully in favor of (very) LATE TERM ABORTION, right up until the time of birth, and beyond - which would be execution. Biden even endorsed the Governor of Virginia, who stated this clearly for all to hear. GET OUT & VOTE!!!" (October 2020)

"The Unsolicited Mail In Ballot Scam is a major threat to our Democracy, & the Democrats know it. Almost all recent elections using this system, even though much smaller & with far fewer Ballots to count, have ended up being a disaster. Large numbers of missing Ballots & Fraud!" (September 2020)

"The Democrats are just ANGRY that the vaccine and delivery are so far ahead of schedule. They hate what they are seeing. Saving lives should make them happy, not sad!" (September 2020)

"Democrats, OPEN THE SCHOOLS (SAFELY), NOW! When schools are closed, let the money follow the child

(FAMILY). Why should schools be paid when they are closed? They shouldn't!" (September 2020)

"Biden and the Democrats want to get rid of the Private Healthcare Plans for 180 MILLION Americans that are happy. They'll be put on socialized medicine!" (September 2020)

"The Democrat Party you once knew — no longer exists!" (October 2020)

"The Democrats are only interested in BAILING OUT their badly managed, high crime, Blue States. They are not interested in our workers or small businesses. Crazy Nancy will only do stimulus, which would be helpful, if we couple it with bailout money. Republican States are great!!!" (September 2020)

"Our Country cannot survive as a Socialist Nation, and that's what the Democrats want it to be..." (October 2020)

"Republicans will be providing far better Healthcare than the Democrats, at a far lower cost...And will always protect people with Pre-existing conditions!!!!" (October 2020)

"Ari, THE MEDIA IS CORRUPT, JUST LIKE OUR DEMOCRAT RUN BALLOT SYSTEM IS CORRUPT! Look at what's happening with Fake, Missing and Fraudulent Ballots all over the Country??? VOTE" (October 2020)

"Joe Biden and the Democrat Socialists will kill your jobs, dismantle your police departments, dissolve your borders, release criminal aliens, raise your taxes, confiscate your guns, end fracking, destroy your suburbs, and drive God from the public square." (October 2020)

"IF YOU WANT A MASSIVE TAX INCREASE, THE BIGGEST IN THE HISTORY OF OUR COUNTRY (AND ONE THAT WILL SHUT OUR ECONOMY AND JOBS DOWN), VOTE DEMOCRAT!!!" (October 2020)

"The Do Nothing Democrats have gone Crazy. Very bad for USA!" (October 2019)

"Such a disgrace that the Do Nothing Democrats are doing just as their name suggests, Doing Nothing! USMCA anyone?" (October 2019)

"My lawyers should sue the Democrats and Shifty Adam Schiff for fraud!" (October 2019)

"Virginia has the best Unemployment and Economic numbers in the history of the State. If the Democrats get in, those numbers will go rapidly in the other direction. On Tuesday, Vote Republican!" (November 2019)

"The Impeachment Hoax is hurting our Stock Market. The Do Nothing Democrats don't care!" (October 2019)

"Republicans are going to fight harder than ever to win back the House because of what the Do Nothing Democrats have done to our Country!" (October 2019)

"So some day, if a Democrat becomes President and the Republicans win the House, even by a tiny margin, they can impeach the President, without due process or fairness or any legal rights. All Republicans must remember what they are witnessing here - a lynching. But we will WIN!" (October 2019)

"Another Record Stock Market, 21 times this year, despite an ongoing, & totally unfounded, Witch Hunt, & a Democrat Party that would love to see a nice, big, juicy recession. In actuality, the potential for the United States is unlimited. We will power through the Do Nothing Dems!" (November 2019)

"What I said on the phone call with the Ukrainian President is "perfectly" stated. There is no reason to call witnesses to analyze my words and meaning. This is just another Democrat Hoax that I have had to live with from the day I got elected (and before!). Disgraceful!" (November 2019)

"If you want to protect criminal aliens – VOTE DEMOCRAT. If you want to protect Law-Abiding Americans – VOTE REPUBLICAN!" (November 2018)

"Republicans will totally protect people with Pre-Existing Conditions, Democrats will not! Vote Republican." (October 2018)

"The only "Collusion" is that of the Democrats with Russia and many others. Why didn't the FBI take the Server from the DNC? They still don't have it. Check out how biased Facebook, Google and Twitter are in favor of the Democrats. That's the real Collusion!" (November 2018)

"If the Democrats think they are going to waste Taxpayer Money investigating us at the House level, then we will likewise be forced to consider investigating them for all of the leaks of Classified Information, and much else, at the Senate level. Two can play that game!" (November 2018)

" ....Where is the DNC Server, and why didn't the FBI take possession of it? Deep State? " (July 2018)

"Is it true the DNC would not allow the FBI access to check server or other equipment after learning it was hacked? Can that be possible?" (March 2017)

"Why didn't the 13 Angry Democrats investigate the campaign of Crooked Hillary Clinton, many crimes, much Collusion with Russia? Why didn't the FBI take the Server from the DNC? Rigged Investigation!" (May 2018)

"Just won lawsuit filed by the DNC and a bunch of Democrat crazies trying to claim the Trump Campaign (and others), colluded with Russia. They haven't figured out that this was an excuse for them losing the election!" (July 2018)

"The Rigged Witch Hunt, originally headed by FBI lover boy Peter S (for one year) & now, 13 Angry Democrats, should look into the missing DNC Server, Crooked Hillary's illegally deleted Emails, the Pakistani Fraudster, Uranium

One, Podesta & so much more. It's a Democrat Con Job!"
(July 2018)

"Russia continues to say they had nothing to do with Meddling in our Election! Where is the DNC Server, and why didn't Shady James Comey and the now disgraced FBI agents take and closely examine it? Why isn't Hillary/Russia being looked at? So many questions, so much corruption!" (June 2018)

""Hillary Clinton and the DNC paid for information from the Russian government to use against her government - there's no doubt about that!" @TuckerCarlson" (August, 2018)

"HOUSE REPUBLICANS SHOULD PASS THE STRONG BUT FAIR IMMIGRATION BILL, KNOWN AS GOODLATTE II, IN THEIR AFTERNOON VOTE TODAY, EVEN THOUGH THE DEMS WON'T LET IT PASS IN THE SENATE. PASSAGE WILL SHOW THAT WE WANT STRONG BORDERS & SECURITY WHILE THE DEMS WANT OPEN BORDERS = CRIME. WIN!" (June 2018)

"It is the Democrats fault for being weak and ineffective with Boarder Security and Crime. Tell them to start thinking about the people devastated by Crime coming from illegal immigration. Change the laws!" (June 2018)

"It's the Democrats fault, they won't give us the votes needed to pass good immigration legislation. They want open borders, which breeds horrible crime. Republicans want security. But I am working on something - it never ends!" (June 2018)

"Why don't the Democrats give us the votes to fix the world's worst immigration laws? Where is the outcry for the killings and crime being caused by gangs and thugs, including MS-13, coming into our country illegally?" (June 2018)

"The Democrats made up and pushed the Russian story as an excuse for running a terrible campaign. Big advantage in Electoral College & lost!" (March 2017)

TRUMP ON MINORITIES

"I'm the least anti-semitic person that you've ever seen in your entire life" (February 2017)

"The Black community brilliantly turned their backs on Mini Mike because they know he is a pandering phony who never did right by them" (March 2020)

"Sleepy Joe Biden has spent 47 years in politics being terrible to Hispanics. Now he is relying on Castro lover Bernie Sanders to help him out. That won't work! Remember, Miami Cubans gave me the highly honored Bay of Pigs Award for all I have done for our great Cuban Population!" (September 2020)

"My #AmericanDreamPlan is a promise to Hispanic Americans to fuel a thriving economy, provide education opportunity for all, preserve freedom, and support faith, family, and community!" (November 2020)

"For 47 years, Sleepy Joe Biden betrayed Hispanic-Americans. Now he wants to close your small businesses, eliminate school choice, and attack our Hispanic Law Enforcement Heroes. I will always stand with the incredible Hispanic-American community!" (November 2020)

"Whether you are African-American, Hispanic-American or ANY AMERICAN at all – you have the right to live in a Country that puts YOUR NEEDS FIRST!" (October 2018)

"African American unemployment is the lowest ever recorded in our country. The Hispanic unemployment rate dropped a full point in the last year and is close to the lowest in recorded history. Dems did nothing for you but get your vote!" (January 2018)

"Kanye West has performed a great service to the Black Community - Big things are happening and eyes are being opened for the first time in Decades - Legacy Stuff!..." (April 2018)

"My Admin has done more for the Black Community than any President since Abraham Lincoln. Passed Opportunity Zones with @SenatorTimScott, guaranteed funding for HBCU's, School Choice, passed Criminal Justice Reform, lowest Black unemployment, poverty, and crime rates in history" (June 2020)

"It is very important that we totally protect our Asian American community in the United States, and all around the world..." (March 2020)

"Asian Americans are VERY angry at what China has done to our Country, and the World. Chinese Americans are the most angry of all. I don't blame them!" (May 2020)

"Those Tweets were NOT Racist. I don't have a Racist bone in my body! The so-called vote to be taken is a Democrat con game. Republicans should not show "weakness" and fall into their trap. This should be a vote on the filthy language, statements and lies told by the Democrat..." (July 2019)

"CNN's Don Lemon, the dumbest man on television, insinuated last night while asking a debate "question" that I was a racist, when in fact I am "the least racist person in the world." Perhaps someone should explain to Don that he is supposed to be neutral, unbiased & fair,....." (July 2019)

"...And I am the least racist person. Black, Hispanic and Asian Unemployment is the lowest (BEST) in the history of the United States!" (August 2019)

"Look forward to being with our great India loving community!" (September 2019)

"Crazy Bernie and the Democrats should see this. I have done far more for the African American community than any President. Secured funding for HBCUs, Criminal Justice Reform, Opportunity Zones, School Choice, Record Low Unemployment, and so much more. THE BEST IS YET TO COME!" (February 2020)

"...I will always stand with the incredible Hispanic-American community!" (November 2020)

TRUMP ON THE SECOND AMENDMENT

"Do you notice we are not having a gun debate right now?
That's because they used knives and a truck!" (June 2017)

"I never said "give teachers guns" like was stated on Fake
News @CNN & @NBC . What I said was to look at the
possibility of giving "concealed guns to gun adept teachers
with military or special training experience - only the
best...." (February 2018)

"Can you imagine what the outcry would be if
@SnoopDogg , failing career and all, had aimed and fired
the gun at President Obama? Jail time!" (March 2017)

"Many ideas, some good & some not so good, emerged
from our bipartisan meeting on school safety yesterday at
the White House. Background Checks a big part of
conversation. Gun free zones are proven targets of killers.
After many years, a Bill should emerge. Respect 2nd
Amendment!" (March 2018)

"....History shows that a school shooting lasts, on average, 3 minutes. It takes police & first responders approximately 5 to 8 minutes to get to site of crime. Highly trained, gun adept, teachers/coaches would solve the problem instantly, before police arrive. GREAT DETERRENT!" (February 2018)

"...immediately fire back if a savage sicko came to a school with bad intentions. Highly trained teachers would also serve as a deterrent to the cowards that do this. Far more assets at much less cost than guards. A "gun free" school is a magnet for bad people. ATTACKS WOULD END!" (February 2018)

"If schools are mandated to be gun free zones, violence and danger are given an open invitation to enter. Almost all school shootings are in gun free zones. Cowards will only go where there is no deterrent!" (March 2018)

"Ralph Northam will allow crime to be rampant in Virginia. He's weak on crime, weak on our GREAT VETS, Anti-Second Amendment...." (November 2017)

"THE SECOND AMENDMENT WILL NEVER BE REPEALED! As much as Democrats would like to see this happen, and despite the words yesterday of former Supreme Court Justice Stevens, NO WAY. We need more Republicans in 2018 and must ALWAYS hold the Supreme Court!" (March 2018)

Made in the USA
Coppell, TX
08 November 2024

39862071R00074